ISBN 978-1-333-59508-1
PIBN 10524160

1 MONTH OF
FREE
READING

at
www.ForgottenBooks.com

By purchasing this book you are eligible for one month membership to ForgottenBooks.com, giving you unlimited access to our entire collection of over 1,000,000 titles via our web site and mobile apps.

To claim your free month visit:
www.forgottenbooks.com/free524160

Reprinted from the *Hindustan Review*, September an October 1909.

THE ISLAM OF MOHAMED.

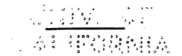

BY

MR. SALAHUDDIN KHUDA BUKHSH, M.A., B.C.I.

BAR-AT-LAW.

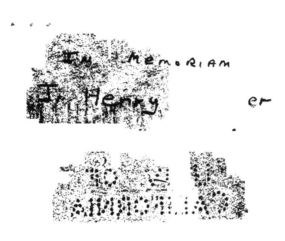

IN MEMORIAM

Fr. Henry

THE ISLAM OF MOHAMED.

By Mr. Salahuddin Khuda Bukhsh, m. a., b. c. l.,
Bar-at-Law.

I.

I DO not desire to explain the importance and significance of Islam among the religious systems of the world ; nor am I to fix and ascertain the exact position of Mohamed as a religious teacher among the world's great teachers of religions. My effort in this paper is simpler and yet not altogether free from bewildering perplexities. I desire to explain what Islam is and what its teachings are : Islam as preached and delivered by the prophet of Arabia ; Islam stripped of the accretions of ages of theological disputes and controversies ; in other words to sketch out, to the best of my light and leading, Islam of the prophet Mohamed. Difficult though this task is, it is not indeed a hopeless venture for one who has kept himself clear and free from narrow sectarianism.

To fully appreciate the message of Mohamed, it is essential that I should say something about the condition of Arabia before Islam. I must readily admit that so far as the Pagan Arabia is concerned, we are in great dearth of authorities. Our information is shadowy, fitful, and fragmentary and the industry of European scholars (such as Caussin De Perceval, Krehl, Wellhausen, Robertson Smith and Sir Charles Lyall) has succeeded but in lifting the veil merely at its fringe. But however partial and unsatisfactory as the account is, of the Pagan days; we can yet form an idea of the life that the Pagan Arabs led and the thoughts that swayed and animated their conduct and their deeds. I will, therefore; describe " The Pre-Islamic Arabia " as briefly as I can.

The Pre-Islamic Arabs were not a nation. Of the sense of nationality, indeed, they had not the vaguest conception, though they were linked by community of speech. Arabia was a sum-total of loose and disconnected congeries of tribes and the tribe was the source and the limit of social and political obligation. Beyond the tribe there lay no duty and no obligation either. Political relations were moral ; for morality was confined within the limits of the tribe. Political organisation was represented by the corporate feeling which found expression in the exercise of the duties of brotherhood. Within the pale of the tribe obtained the prohibition to kill, to commit adultery, to steal, &c., &c. Beyond it there was no such prohibition. Fidelity to one's kinsman was an imperative duty, apart from any question of the justness of the cause.* Outside the tribe there was nothing but constant plunder and unceasing warfare. "Certain large groups were, indeed, almost continually at war with one another. Ma'add, the people of the Hijaz and Al-yamamah generally looked upon Al-yaman as their natural prey and were constantly raiding on the herds of their southern neighbours. Between Tamim and Bakr, son of Wail, there was permanent bad blood. Ghatafan and Hawazin had a standing feud. In the north the kingdom of Al-Hirah, the representative of Persian predominance was the hereditary enemy of Ghassan, the representative of the might of Rome." (Lyall, *Ancient Arabian Poetry, p.* xxiii.) Arabia, before Islam, was thus a theatre of internecine warfare, restrained, but partially, by the introduction of blood money. There was compensation for everything for which vengeance could be exacted. All crimes were assessed as economic damage. Every loss of honor, property, or life could be appraised by agreement ; all having their price in camels. We thus see that the Arabs before Islam had scarcely emerged from barbaric conditions. † There was no social order, no organised government. The law of sheer brute force prevailed, untempered and unrestrained, by any civilizing or controlling influence. Nor did they attain any refined idea of religion. Their religion was nothing more or less than gross fetichism ; the worship of tree and stone, the veneration of certain personified divine attributes, meaningless ritual and ceremonials. The true religious spirit they never succeeded in grasping and the fear of God never exercised any real, practical influence over their conduct and actions. It was reserved for Islam to instil into them the sense of responsibility to God and to make this idea of human responsibility the guiding and controlling principle of life. To all appearance the Arabs honoured the gods, went on pilgrimage to

---

* Wellhausen, *Reste Arabischen Heidentums*, p. 226.

† I have avoided further details here, as I have dealt with this subject, at length, in my *Contributions to the History of Islamic Civilisation*, pp. 146—169.

their sanctuaries, made sacrifices in the temples, anointed with the blood of the victims gods carved out of stone or made of wood, consulted the oracles, when in difficulty, and questioned them about the future. But all this was sham and counterfeit. Of real, genuine, religious feeling there was none. This empty show, however, was kept up for purposes of gain; the manifold sanctuaries yielding large incomes to certain noble families and clans. *

In a soil, apparently so uncongenial, how did Islam strike its root? This is an interesting and fascinating question and we must try to solve it here. The solution of this question is to be found in the existence of Judaism and Christianity, on the one hand, and in the commercial activity of the Arabs, on the other. By commerce the Arabs acquired an extended knowledge of foreign nations and their civilisation. Frequent contact with the outer world widened their intellectual horizon and awakened in them higher and more spiritual thoughts. They learnt new ideas, acquired new habits and, what was most valuable of all, they learnt to think for themselves. But not merely did travel in foreign countries and intercourse with foreign people exercise a disruptive influence, but there were forces, alike subversive and destructive, nearer home. In Arabia itself the two streams of Christianity and Judaism flowed, side by side, with the Arab Heathenism.

That Christianity had made a considerable advance among the Arabs is clear from the fact, that, at the time of Mohamed, it was considerably diffused not merely among the Rabia tribes but even among the Tamim. Nor did the Taiyy altogether escape its influence. Its growth, however, was not so favourable in Hijaz and central Arabia, but even here Christian ideas undoubtedly made their way through commerce and social intercourse. Similarly the Jewish influence was equally powerful. When the Jews came to Arabia we do not definitely know, but Dr. Noldeke points out that a great Jewish immigration into Arabia cannot be fixed prior to the destruction of Jerusalem by Titus and Hadrian. At all events, it is clear that at the time of Mohamed

---

* Deutsch, *Literary Remains*, p. 87. For further information see Von per, *Culturgeschichtliche Streifzuge* (my translation, p. 49.)

there was a large colony of Jews at Taima, Khaibar, Yathrib, Fedak and Yaman. They did not live scattered amidst Arab population but kept together and, though despised by the Ara'sq they were yet indispensible to them as merchants, jewellers, and goldsmiths. It would, therefore, be not an error to suppose that they exerted no small spiritual influence over the Arabs.[*] That this is no unfounded theory or improbable supposition is evidenced by the fact that in the works of four of the most prominent Arabian poets of the Pre-Islamic time—An-Nabigah, Zuhair, Al-Asha and Labid—we find expressions which show that they, at least, if not the wild wanderers of the desert, knew very well what a spiritual religion meant.[†] Ibn Qutaibah enumerates drinking, joy, wrath and love among the "motive causes" which speed the poet but we cannot fail to detect in their poems an undercurrent of deep religious feelings. Individual minds felt a sense of uneasiness and sought to find some plausible solution of the mysteries of life and death and traces of such a frame of mind we notice frequently in ancient Arab poetry. On no other basis, indeed, can we explain away the lamentations of the royal poet Imra-ul-Qais over the worthlessness of the life of pleasure that he had led and the conversion to Christianity of Qais B. Zuhair, the leader of the Abs in the long fratricidal war against the Dhubian.[‡] In considering the rise of Islam we cannot be unwatchful of the course of contemporary thought or unmindful of the religious forces which contributed to its success. Such, indeed, were the forces at work in Arabia before Mohamed ; forces which could not have failed to stir higher thoughts in enlightened minds and to create a reaction against the Arab Heathenism. And a reaction, indeed, did set in. A band of distinguished men, whom we must recognise as the heralds and standard-bearers of Islam, no longer willing to tolerate idolatorous practices, definitely cut themselves adrift from the Arabian Paganism. They called themselves Hanifs ; a word of doubtful meaning and the cause of much controversy. "The most acceptable conjecture seems to me", says Sir Charles Lyall, "to be that of Sprenger that it is connected with the Hebrew HANEF heretic." Hanifism had certain specific features : rejection of idolatory, abstention from certain kinds of food, and the worship of "the

---

[*] Wellhausen, *Reste*, pp. 230-231. [†] Lyall, *Ancient Arabian Poetry*, p. 93.
[‡] In Wellhausen's *Reste* p. 229 will be found the passage in question from Imra-ul-Qais.

God of Abraham." Ascetic practices, such as the wearing of
sackcloth, are also ascribed to some of the Hanifs. * Islamic
tradition has handed down to us the names of a number of religious
thinkers before Mohamed, who are described as Hanifs and of
whom the following is a list :—

1. Warakah b. Naufal of Kuraish. 2. Ubaidulla b. Jahsh. 3. Uthman b.
Al Huwarith. 4. Zaid b.' Amr b. Naufal.

Ibn Kutaibah adds to the above :—

5. Urbab b. al Bara' of Abdul Qais 6. Umayyah b. Abi-s-Salt. 7. Kuss b.
Saidah of Iyad (Aghani XIV, 41-44) Mohamed heard him at Ukaidh but he
died before the mission. 8. Abu Kais Sirnrah b. Abi Anas. 9. Khalid b.
Sinan b. Ghaith of Abs.

To these Sir Charles Lyall adds :—

10. Abu Kais Saifi, Ibn Al-Aslat of the Aus-allah of Yathrib.

It is impossible to misconceive the importance and significance of Hanifism in the origin of Islam. The path was
already prepared for it and Islam offered to the Arabs what they
were long in search for : a moral, ethical, and spiritual teaching ;
a higher form of worship and last but not least fraternity and union.
The tribal cults were henceforward merged in a higher worship
and the nobler energies of .the Arab race obtained a religious
consecration.

Islam became the starting point for the Arabs for conquests,
alike spiritual and temporal. With Islam became the preroga-
tive of the Arab race to be "an ensign to the nations ;" to bear
and to carry the banner of the true God to the remotest corner
of the earth. Hence the unceasing campaigns and hence the
far-extending conquests.

II.

It is clear beyond doubt that Christian and Jewish influences,
to a large extent, unsettled and disturbed the beliefs of the
Pagan Arabs and paved the way for the prophet. Resistance
to his faith there was, but it was resistance on the part of those,
who sought to maintain the old faith and superstition ; not on
account of any warmth of conviction or sincerety of zeal, but on
account of the fear and apprehension that the success of Islam
would mean loss of large incomes derived from the temples and

* Journal of the Asiatic Society October, 1903 p. 773. Khuda Bukhsh, *Islamic
Civilisation* p. 147 and the authorities therein cited.

old heathen practices. * But resistance, founded upon such a selfish basis, could not prevent, and indeed did not prevent, the onward progress of Islam. In the deadly conflict between Islam and the Arab Heathenism Islam triumphed.

We, now, proceed to enquire as to what was the basis or, in other words, what were the sources from which Islam was derived. Islam freely borrowed from Judaism and Christianity and even did not hesitate to adopt practices prevalent in Pre-Islamic Arabia. In fashioning his religion the prophet adopted an eclectic method, retaining or rejecting from the older systems whatever seemed to him necessary and proper. It is not exactly within the scope of my paper to precisely specify or to accurately define the exact obligation of Islam to Christianity or Judaism. Such a discussion would take me far afield. Professor Wellhausen is inclined to belittle the influence of Judaism in the birth and infancy of Islam and points to the Islamic conception of Jesus, as the greatest of the prophets before Mohamed, as a conclusive proof of his contention. But the present writer is not prepared to attach much weight to this argument. If the Islamic conception of Jesus, indeed, is to be put forward as indicating the absence of Judaic influence on early Islam ; with equal force might the Islamic conception of Jesus be urged as subversive of the theory of Christian influence, so stoutly advocated by Professor Wellhausen. † The basis of dogmatic Christianity, namely, the sonship of Christ, Mohamed inveighed against early and late. It would be idle to deny the indebtedness of Islam to Judaism. Mohamed has not merely accepted dogmas and doctrines of Judaism, minute Talmudical ordinances, but has even adopted, in its entirety, some of the Jewish practices and, far above all these, that which indeed constitutes the very foundation of Islam, namely, the conception of a severe and uncompromising monotheism. ‡ The fact is that both Judaism and Christianity were used and used freely by the prophet in building up his religion. Nor is this a new theory. The prophet never put him-

* Von Kremer, *Culturgeschichte des orients*, p. 24, vol. I
† Wellhausen pp. 236 ct. Seq. Prof. Wellhausen admits Jewish influence in the Islamic theocracy and in the belief that the prophet, as representative of God, is alone entitled to rule and govern, to the exclusion of all other powers. See, also Deutsch p. 171.
‡ See the learned monograph of Geiger, *Was hat Mohammed ans Judenthume aufgenommen.*

self forward as introducing something new but he invariably claimed for himself the honour of reviving the old and the true beliefs which had fallen into neglect and oblivion. But besides the Jewish and Christian sources, not a small portion of Islamic ritual and ceremonials were mere reproductions of Pre-Islamic practices. The entire ceremonies relating to the pilgrimage (Hajj) and the sacred service, at the temple of Mecca, have survived in Islam with little or no variation from the days of Arab Heathenism ; * the only change that Mohamed effected in them was to allow the pilgrims to put on a particular pilgrim dress consisting of two pieces of cloth of which one covers the hip and the other breast and shoulders ; while the head has to be kept uncovered, as in ancient days, when they used to make up their hair into a sort of wig by means of some glutinous substance. And so indeed it has remained, to this day, the prescribed pilgrim costume. After visiting the Kabah they used, in heathen days, to visit the two rocky hills of Safa and Merwah on which were placed two bronze idols. Mohamed went so far in his toleration of the heathen pilgrimage customs that he suffered the visit to Safa and Marwah to continue as before, but had the two idols removed. Of the history of the origin of the forms of the prayer, prostration, ablution, and fasts our knowledge is vague, uncertain and shadowy.

Islam has, says Von Kremer,

largely drawn upon Judaism, Christianity, the religion of Zoroaster and possibly even from Manichenism. From Parsiism it has taken both directly and indirectly. A number of obviously Parsi ideas have penetrated into Islam through the channel of Jewish books ; notably the Talmud. The doctrine of the resurrection, most of the legends relating to heaven and hell, and the entire system of demonology have found their way into the Qur'an through Judaism. So indeed did the description of the trial and the tortures of the dead in the grave by two angels *Munkar* and *Nakir*. The idea of the bridge *sirat* as thin as a hair, which leads to paradise across the abyss of hell is certainly derived from the Parsis ; having passed over into the Qur'an through the Midrash. But Islam has not hesitated to borrow directly from Parsiism. It is a significant fact that the word *din*, which so repeatedly occurs in the Qur'an, has been borrowed from the Parsi books. In the Huzveresh it appears in exactly the same form (old Backtrian dæna).*

___

* Lyall, p. 93 ; Von Kremer's *Culturgeschichtliche Streifzuge* (my translation p. 47). The author of Ras' Mal-in-Nadim, (Bankipore, M.S.) gives an account of Heathen practices (Fol. 17et Seq) ; specially drawing attention to those retained by Islam.

It is not suggested that the prophet had access to the written books of either the Jews or the Christians; though in some passages of the Qur'an we can trace direct resemblances to the text of the Old Testament and the Mishna.* His knowledge of the Jewish and Christian books, at times faulty and imperfect to a degree, was derived almost exclusively by oral communications.

I trust I have said enough to illustrate the condition of Arabia before Islam and the sources from which the prophet of Arabia received his religious inspiration. I, now, go on to explain Islam and its tenets.

III.

Mr. Ameer Ali explains Islam as "striving after righteousness," but Prof. Hirschfeld, in his luminous *Researches into the Composition and Exegesis of the Qur'an*, very correctly points out that Mr. Ameer Ali's definition only reflects the theoretical and moral side of the question—limited to the initial stage of Islam. †

The term Islam, as time went by, included the whole of the theoretical and practical constitution of the faith and as such it is interpreted by Al-Ghazzali in his Ibya-ul-ulum (P. 104, vol. I. Islam, says he, is an expression for submission and unquestioning obedience, abandonment of insubordination, defiance and opposition. And it is in this light, indeed, that the prophet himself regarded Islam. "The Bedwins say: (XLIX. 14) we believe," Speak ! you shall not "believe" (only, but say we practice Islam (Aslamna). In Surah III. 17 (Cf. V. 79) Islam is identified with *din* (Cf. LXI. 7-9) and the relation between the two synonyms, says Prof. Hirschfeld, is broadly discussed by Al-Shahrastani (Milal, pp. 25 to 27) and is stated to embrace the five duties, *viz.* :—Of testifying to the unity of God and the Divine inspiration of Mohamed, the duties of reciting prayers, giving alms, fasting in the *Ramadhan*, and performing the pilgrimage to Mecca. The fundamental basis of Islam is the unity of God ; stern, unbending monotheism and this doctrine of the unity of God is proclaimed in the Qur'an,

---

* Von Kremer, *Culturgeschichtliche Streifzüge* (my translation p. 47) Comp. Qur'an XXI, 105 with PS XXX VII 29 ; 1-5 with Ps. XXVII. The New Testament. Comp. VII, 48 with Luke XVI. 24 ; XLVI, 19 with Luke XVI. 25. Then again verse 35 corresponds almost word for word with Mishna Sanh IV. 5 ; also II. 183 with Mishna Ber. 1.2. Noldeke, *Sketches from Eastern History*, p. 31.

† *Life and Teachings of Mohamed* p. 226 Prof. Hirschfeld p. 14.

in season and out of season and ever and anon with augmented emphasis. To associate gods with God is the most unpardonable sin and the prophet's extensive vocabulary of vituperation is never exhausted in attacking those who associate gods with God. In Surah VI (verses 74-79) we have one of the most charming passages testifying to the unity of God :—

And remember when Abraham said to his father, Azar, thou takest those images as God ? verily I see that thou and thy people are in manifest error.

And so did we show Abraham the domain of the heavens and of the earth that he might be one of those who are established in knowledge. And when the night over-shadowed him he beheld a star " This, said he, is My Lord " but when it set, he cried, " I love not gods which set." And when he beheld the moon uprising " This," said he, " is my Lord " but when it set, he said, " surely, if My Lord guide me not I shall be of those who go astray."

And when he beheld the Sun uprise, he said, " This is my Lord," " this is the greatest " but when it set, he said " O my people I share not with you the guilt of joining gods with God."

I verily turn my face to him who hath created the Heavens and the earth following the right religion and I am not one of those who add gods to God."

Not a whit has Gibbon* exaggerated the truth when he wrote " the creed of Mohamed is free from suspicion or ambiguity and the Qur'an is a glorious testimony to the unity of God. The prophet of Mecca rejected the worship of idols and men, of stars and planets, on the rational principle that whatever is born must die, that whatever is corruptible must decay and perish." And, again, says the historian of the Roman Empire, " these sublime truths, thus announced in the language of the prophet, are firmly held by his disciples and defined with metaphysical precision by the interpreters of the Qur'an. A philosophic atheist might subscribe the popular creed of Mohamedans : a creed too sublime perhaps for our present faculties."

The unity of God, therefore, is the central faith of Islam and connected with it, by natural process as it were, is the belief that man is responsible to the creator for his actions and deeds. This belief, the Pre-Islamic Arab never knew or conceived, and the prophet Mohamed, by inculcating this belief, not only laid the foundation of a spiritual life among his countrymen, but laid the foundation of a well-organized society ; soon destined to grow into a magnificent empire. The sphere of duty and

---

* Gibbon, Bury's Ed. Vol V p. 339.

obligation, charity and sympathy, confined hitherto merely to tribesmen, was widened and extended and the narrow tribal tie was lost in the larger brotherhood of faith. At this distance of time, it is perhaps difficult for us to fully realize the influence of this teaching, but to it alone must we ascribe the dethronement of those ideals of Arabian Paganism which the author of the *Muhummedanische Studien* has so graphically described, comparing and contrasting them with the higher ideals substituted by Islam.* The religion of the prophet, like the wand of a magician, completely and utterly changed the life of the Arabs. It hushed their tribal disputes into silence, it destroyed their insularity, it set up a purer and a more refined standard of domestic life, it opened before them fresh vistas of spiritual happiness and temporal success.

Next to the unity of God, Islam enjoins five daily prayers upon its followers. It is curious that the Qur'an lays down no rule as to the manner in which the prayer should be offered. Apparently, as Mr. Ameer Ali† points out, the practice of the prophet has associated certain rights and ceremonies to the due observance of prayers. In the Mohamedan prayer we observe the Jewish practice of standing erect, the Christian of prostration and a third of inclination.‡ Orginally the prophet instituted three daily prayers.§ Their extension to five was an innovation of the late Meccan period; the details of the purity legislation appear to have still later. " Yet the theory," says Prof. Margoliouth, " that God should be approached only by persons in a state of purity was known in South Arabia before Mohamed's time, whence it is probable that his earliest converts were instructed therein."

Prayers are to be performed five times in course of every day: between daybreak and sunrise, between noon and the "asr" (which later period is about mid-time between noon and nightfall) between the " asr " and sunset, between sunset and the " asha " (or the period when the darkness of night commences) and at, or after the " asha." ‖It is considered more meritorious to take part in the public *salat* of the community conducted by a leader (Imam) than

---

* Goldziher, *Muhammedanische Studien.* Vol I. The chapter on Muruwwa und Din ; Nicholson, *Literary History of the Arabs* pp. 177-179 ; Browne *Literary History of Persia* pp. 189 et Seq. † *Life and Teachings of Mohamed* p. 263 ‡ Margoliouth *Life of Mohamed* p. 102 § Ibn Sad, Vol. IV. Part I. p. 159.

to discharge the *salat* by oneself. Von Kremer has rightly emphasised the importance of the Muslim prayer by recognizing the mosque as the drill ground for the warlike believers of early Islam. In stern discipline, in unconditional obedience, says Von Kremer, the author of the *Culturgeschichite des orients*, lay the greatest achievement of Mohamed and the real secret of the strength of Islam. ¶ The five daily prayers where the leader (the Imam) stood before the community, closely arrayed behind him, and where every movement of his was imitated with military preciseness, by the hundreds of the faithful assembled in the mosque, served, among the Muslims, in those times, the purpose of that what is known now as the drill ground : a school where the people learnt to assemble, to move in a body and to follow the Commander.

In the Qur'an *the command to pay the poor-tax (zakat) directly follows the command to pray : perform the prayers and pay the poor-tax. This tax had a strong communistic complexion which is evidenced by the following tradition : " The prophet sent Ma'dh to Yaman and told him : summon them to accept the confession of faith namely, there is no God but Allah and I that am his prophet ; if they listen to it ; teach them further that God has ordained five daily prayers ; if they are also agreeable to this ; teach them further that God has enjoined the poor-tax (sadakah) payable by the wealthy upon their property for distribution among the poor." † This tax was annually payable upon camels, oxen (bulls and cows) and buffalos, sheep and goats, horses and mules and asses and gold and silver (whether in money or ornaments, etc., provided the property was of a certain amount ; as five camels, thirty oxen, forty sheep, five horses, two hundred dirhams, or twenty dinars ‡. The proportion is generally one-fortieth, which is to be paid in kind or in money or other equivalent.

The third most important obligation enjoined by Islam is fasting in the month of *Ramadhan*. The Muslim must abstain from eating and drinking and from every indulgence of the senses, every day during the month of *Ramd'un*, from the first appearance of daybreak until sunset, unless physically incapacitated. The last

---

* In Lane's *Arabian Society in the Middle Ages* the reader will find a detailed account of religious institutions of Islam pp. 1-24. † Vol. I. p. 10. ‡ Surah. 2. 40.

§ Von Kremer, Vol p. 50 † Lane, *Arabian Society* p. 14.

but not least is the pilgrimage to Mecca and mount Arafat, which the Muslim must perform at least once in his life.

These then ; namely, the unity of God, the belief in the Divine mission of the prophet, five daily prayers, fasting in the month of *Ramadhan* and the pilgrimage, are the essentials of Islam. The one supreme mission of the prophet was to create and to maintain an absolute brotherhood in faith. All Muslims were declared equal, irrespective of birth, rank or profession ; and the world has never seen, perhaps, a more perfect democracy than the one called into being by the prophet. Truly, the most worthy of honour in the sight of God, says the Qur'an, is he who feareth Him most ; for the faithful are brethren ; whereupon make peace between your brethren. A similar refrain runs through the parting sermon of the prophet ; "O men ! God has taken away from you the arrogance and pride of ancestry of heathen days. An Arab has no excellence or superiority over a barbarian than that which is secured to him by his God-fearing and righteousness. Ye are all the progeny of Adam, and Adam himself is of the Earth."

No caste and no priestcraft does Islam recognise. Every Muslim is his own priest and every spot of land is his *mosque* to pray and to worship *Allah*. For no other purpose than to keep alive the sense of corporate unity of the Muslims did the prophet declare the superiority of the public prayer over prayer by oneself and establish the institution of pilgrimage.

Year after year, from all parts of the Islamic world, streamed to Mekka, Muslims in thousands and tens of thousands, to worship Allah at the Ka'bah and to perform the *Hajj*. There, at Mekka, year after year, Muslims of divers nationalities recognised and realised the potent spell of their faith and felt more deeply and keenly than ever the tie which bound them together. Moreover, as Von Kremer points out, there did the Muslims obtain an opportunity of listening to the lectures of far-famed professors and men of letters who attracted, year by year, an ever-increasing audience. There indeed, did Islam shine forth in its full lustre ; attracting and alluring, enthralling and captivating its followers, as it could do no where else. Every spot, associated with some historical incident ; every place, connected with some important event or other of the life of the

teacher, awakened the love and fired the enthusiasm of Muslims for the son of Abdullah, the maker of Arabia and the
founder of Islam.

In his fascinating book, *The Life and Teachings of Mohamed,*
Mr. Ameer Ali has admirably summed up the Islamic teachings:—
" Nothing can be simpler or more in accord with the advance of
the human intellect than the teachings of the Arabian prophet.
The few rules for religious ceremonial which he prescribed
were chiefly with the object of maintaining discipline and uni-
formity, so necessary in certain stages of society, but they were
by no means of an inflexible character. He allowed them to be
broken in cases of illness or other causes. ' God wishes to make
things easy for you, for ' says the Qur'an ' man was created weak.'
The legal principles which he enunciated were either delivered
as answers to questions put to him as the Chief Magistrate of
Medina or to remove or correct patent evils. The prophet's
Islam recognized no ritual likely to distract the mind from the
thought of the one God, no law to keep enchained the conscience
of advancing humanity."

Nothing was more distant from the prophet's thought
than to fetter the mind or to lay down fixed, immutable,
unchanging laws for his followers. The Qur'an is a book of
guidance to the faithful and not, to be sure, an obstacle
in the path of their social, moral, legal and intellectual progress.
The requirements of Islam are at once easy and simple and
leave scope to Muslims to take part in their duties as subjects
or citizens ; to attend to their religious obligations without
sacrificing their worldly prosperity and to adopt, whatever is
good, in any community or civilisation, without any interference
on the part of their religion.

IV

I shall now make a few general observations on the religion
of the prophet of Arabia. Whatever Islam may have become
through pharisaic artificiality and theological subtlety, its
leading principles are as broad as the starriest heavens and as
enduring as the everlasting hills. It contains, in common
with other great religions, those eternal truths which are
only too liable to be forgotten in blind zeal, in warmth of

controversy, in sectarian narrow-mindedness, in religious fanaticism, but which our education and culture teach us to discover and appreciate, wherever we find them. The governing principle of all religions is the same. In the language of the apostle James: " Pure religion and undefiled before God and the Father is this ; to visit the fatherless and widows in their affliction and to keep oneself unspotted from the world." This is the burden of all religions and this the burden of Islam.

The kernel and doctrine of Islam, Goethe has found in the second *surah* which begins as follows :—"This is the Book. There is no doubt in the same. A guidance to the righteous, who believe in the unseen, who observe the prayer and who give alms of that which we have vouchsafed unto them. And who believe in that which has been sent down unto thee—(the Revelation) which had been sent down to those before thee, and who believe in the life to come. They walk in the guidance of their Lord, and they are the blessed. As to them who believe not—it is indifferent to them whether thou exhortest them or not exhortest them. They will not believe. Sealed hath Allah their hearts and their ears and over their eye is darkness and theirs will be a great punishment.—" " And in this wise," Goethe continues, " we have *surah* after *surah*. Belief and unbelief are divided into higher and lower. Heaven and hell await the believers or deniers. Detailed injuctions of things allowed and forbidden, legendary stories of Jewish and Christian religion, amplifications of all kinds, boundless tautologies and repetitions, form the body of this sacred volume, which, to us, as often as we approach it, is repellent anew, next attracts us ever anew and fills us with admiration, and finally forces us into veneration."

This passage, indeed, is as good a summary as any other, but there is one, and in this same chapter, still more explicit, illustrating the catholicity of the prophet's mind and his discerning judgment. When Mohamed, says Deutsch*, told his adherents at Medina no longer to turn in prayer towards Jerusalem but towards the Ka'bah at Mekka, to which their fathers had turned, and he was blamed for this innovation he replied :—" That is not

---

* *Literary Remains*, p. 128.

righteousness : whether ye turn your faces towards east or west, God's is the east as well as the west. But verily righteousness is his who believes in God, in the day of judgment, in the angels, in the book and the prophets; who bestows his wealth for God's sake, upon kindred, and orphans, and the poor, and the homeless, and all those who ask; and also upon delivering the captives; he who is steadfast in prayer, giveth alms, who stands firmly by his covenants, when he has once entered into them ; and who is patient in adversity, in hardship and in times of trial. These are the righteous, and these are the God-fearing." What a noble idea of life and religion do we find here. It is not merely the recitation of prayers which constitutes righteousness but in solemnly acting the religion we profess; in tender regard for the poor and the orphan, the forlorn and the suffering ; in relieving the miseries of the captives, in holding by the promises made, in enduring with calm fortitude the trials and reverses of fortune. Here, in this passage, we have the key to Islam, nay, I would go further and say a key to all religions. It is only the clouded vision which sees difference between one religion and the other ; to one who has the eyes to see and the heart to feel, all religions appear as but a reflection of one and the same light.

ماواے ٹر از مسجد و میخانه کام است — اے خانه بران از توا دانہ کدام است
از کثرت روزن نہ شود مہر مکرر — اے کج نظران کعبہ و بتخانه کدام است

This was the spirit of the prophet's religion which he preached in the Qur'an in every accent of pleading and warning, of pathos and hope, of repentance and forgiveness. He stood firm by his faith unshaken by threats and persuasion. His success, indeed, marks the ascent of the soul, of the higher and nobler nature of man from the darkness to the light. Nor was it a different light to that which had appeared to humanity " at sundry times and in divers manners." His preaching fell on the Arabs, still in the spring tide of their national life, and laid a tremendous hold upon their mind and their imagination ; changing and transforming them and giving them as it were, a new existence. It taught them firmness of resolve, contempt of death, singleness of purpose, unity and fraternity, and it gave them that intensity of religious fervour which became the most valued asset of their national life. Above all, says Dr. Noldeke,

Islam gave and gives, to those who profess it a feeling of confidence such as is imparted by hardly any other faith.* And, indeed, it was this, again, which made them great warriors and conquerors of the world.†

Islam possesses an inherent force and vitality which nothing can weaken or destory. It carries within it germs of progress and development and has great powers of adaptability to changing circumstances. There is nothing in its teachings which conflicts with or militates against modern civilisation, and the moment Muslims realise this truth their future will be assured. and their greatness only a question of time. Modern Islam, with its hierarchy of priesthood, gross fanaticism, appalling ignorance and superstitious practices, is, indeed, a discredit to the Islam of the prophet Mohamed. Instead of unity we have Islam torn into factions, instead of culture we have indifference to learning ; instead of liberal-minded. toleration we have gross bigotry. But this intellectual darkness must necessarily be followed by intellectual dawn and we trust, that it is not now far distant or too long to come.

An impartial consideration of the life of the prophet and his teachings cannot fail to awaken the warmest admiration for the man and his mission. Whatever may be the defects in the Qur'an, even non-Muslims must concede that it is a noble testimony to the unity of God and whatever may be the blemishes in the life of the prophet, none, but a perverse mind, will regard him as anything but sincere in his conviction, honest in his purpose and unshaken in his resolve. Mohamedan civilisation was the outcome of Mohamedan faith and nothing but Islam alone can again give to the Mohamedans what they have lost : their civilisation, their culture, and their empire.

* *Sketches from Eastern History*, p. 27.
† Von Kremer, vol. I, p. 92.

The City Press, Allahabad.

CPSIA information can be obtained
at www.ICGtesting.com
Printed in the USA
LVHW010745291118
598533LV00024BA/1327